Water Cycle

Torrey Maloof

Consultants

Sally Creel, Ed.D.
Curriculum Consultant

Leann Iacuone, M.A.T., NBCT, ATC
Riverside Unified School District

Image Credits: p.23 (top) iStock/Getty Images; p.24–25 (background) iStock; p.12 (top right) Kenneth Libbrecht/ Science Source; pp.28–29 (illustrations) J.J. Rudisill; all other images from Shutterstock.

Library of Congress Cataloging-in-Publication Data

Maloof, Torrey, author.
Water cycle / Torrey Maloof ; consultant, Sally Creel, Ed.D., curriculum consultant, Leann Iacuone, M.A.T., NBCT, ATC Riverside Unified School District, Jill Tobin, California Teacher of the Year semi-finalist Burbank Unified School District.
pages cm
Summary: "Every living thing needs water to live. Water is an important part of life. There is water all around us. It moves through the water cycle. It brings water to all parts of the planet."— Provided by publisher.
Audience: K to grade 3.
Includes index.
ISBN 978-1-4807-4612-1 (pbk.)
ISBN 978-1-4807-5079-1 (ebook)
1. Hydrologic cycle—Juvenile literature.
2. Water—Juvenile literature. I. Title.
GB848.M35 2015
551.48—dc23

2014014121

Teacher Created Materials
5301 Oceanus Drive
Huntington Beach, CA 92649-1030
http://www.tcmpub.com

ISBN 978-1-4807-4612-1

Printed by: 51497
Printed in: China

Table of Contents

Water World

Clouds gather. The sky grows dark. The wind whistles. Small drops of rain begin to fall. Then, the large, loud storm begins! Soon, water is everywhere.

When there's a storm, it's easy to find water. But if you look closely, even on a sunny day, there is water all around.

Old Water

Most of the water on Earth is really old. It has been around for billions of years!

Water flows through streams. It runs down rivers. It fills our oceans. Waves of water crash on our beaches.

Water is in plants. Water is in animals. Water is even in you! It is everywhere, and it is on the move.

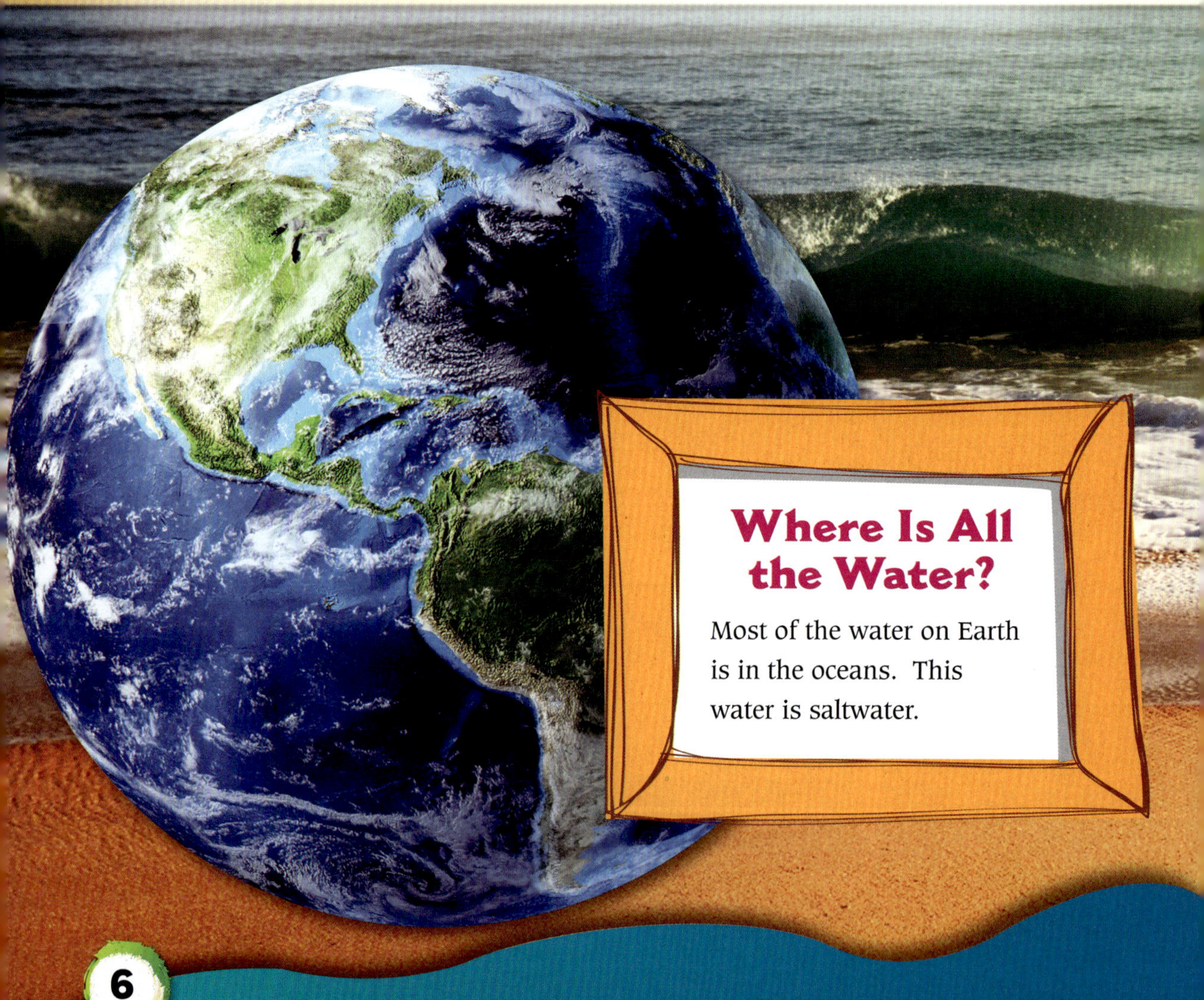

Where Is All the Water?

Most of the water on Earth is in the oceans. This water is saltwater.

a stream

Our bodies are made mostly of water.

Liquid, Solid, Gas

Water moves and changes. It can be a **liquid**. This means it flows freely. The water you drink is a liquid. But if the air gets cold, water can freeze. It turns into a **solid**. Ice is a solid. When liquid water gets hot, it changes again. It turns into a gas. Then, it is called water **vapor**.

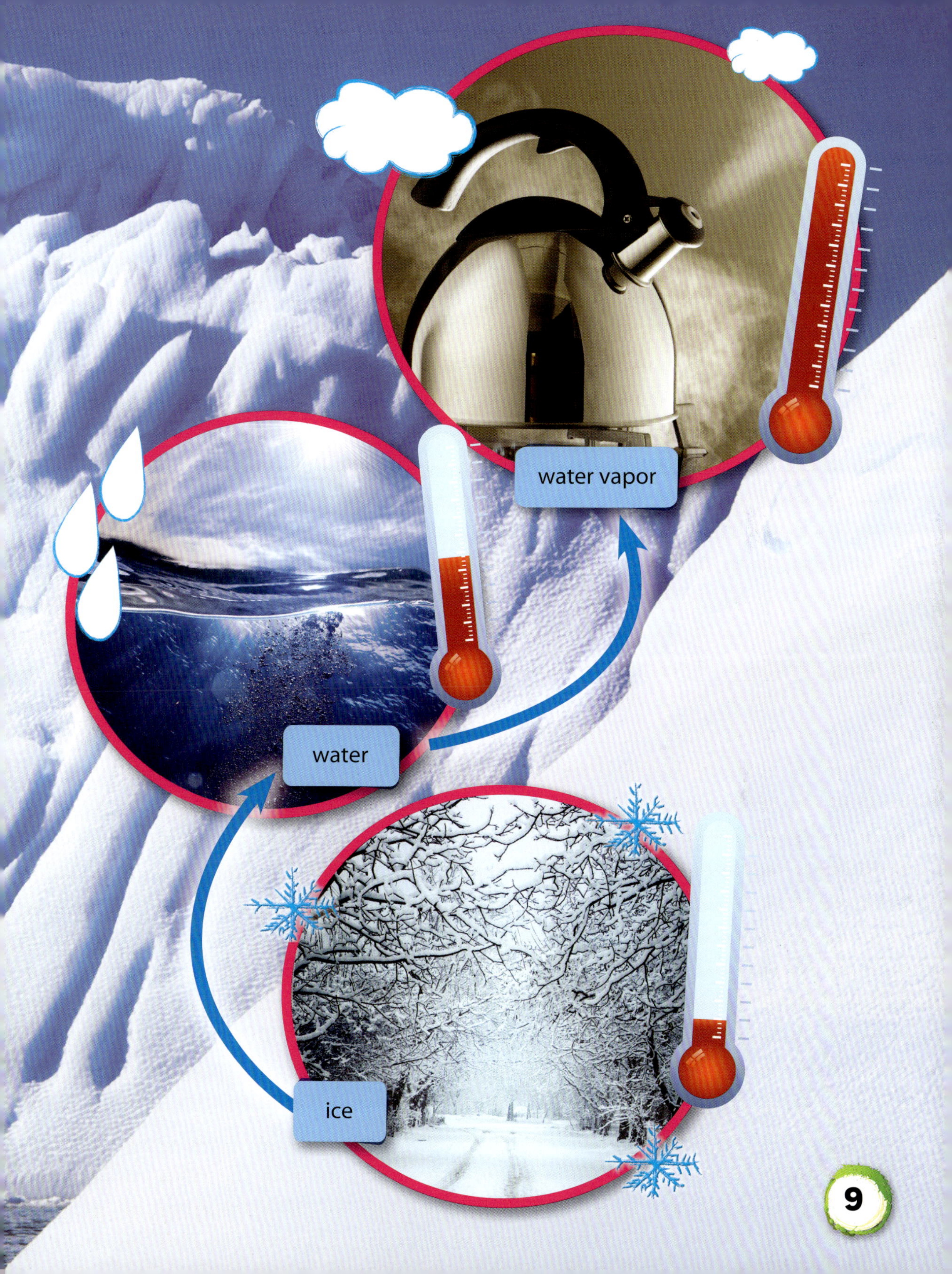
water vapor
water
ice

The Cycle

Some things happen over and over. They occur in the same order. This is called a *cycle*. Water moves in a cycle. There are three parts of the water cycle: **evaporation** (ih-vap-uh-REY-shuhn), **condensation**, and **precipitation**.

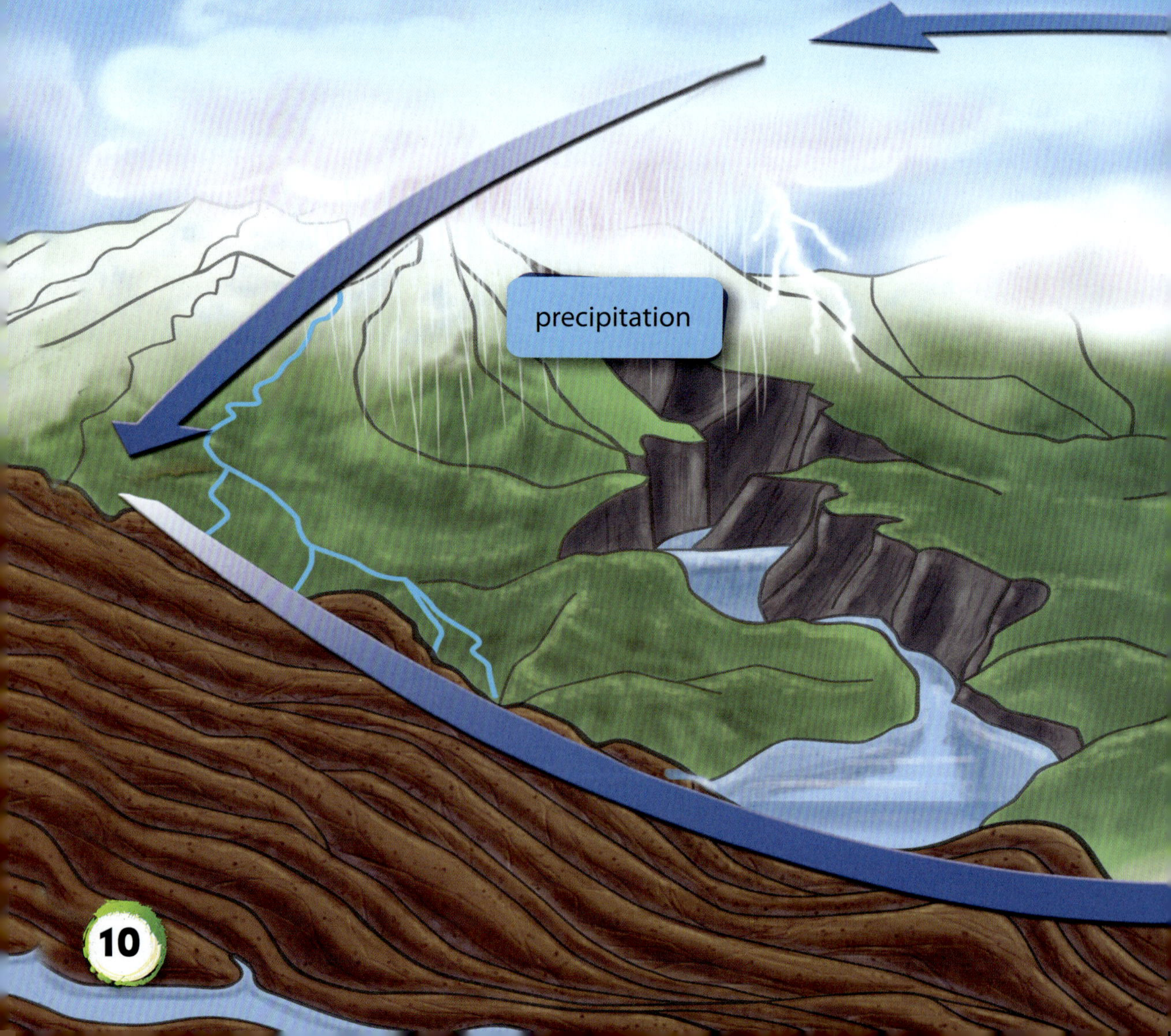

The cycle starts when the sun warms the water. The water evaporates. It turns into vapor. Next, the vapor rises into the air. There, it cools and makes clouds. This is condensation.

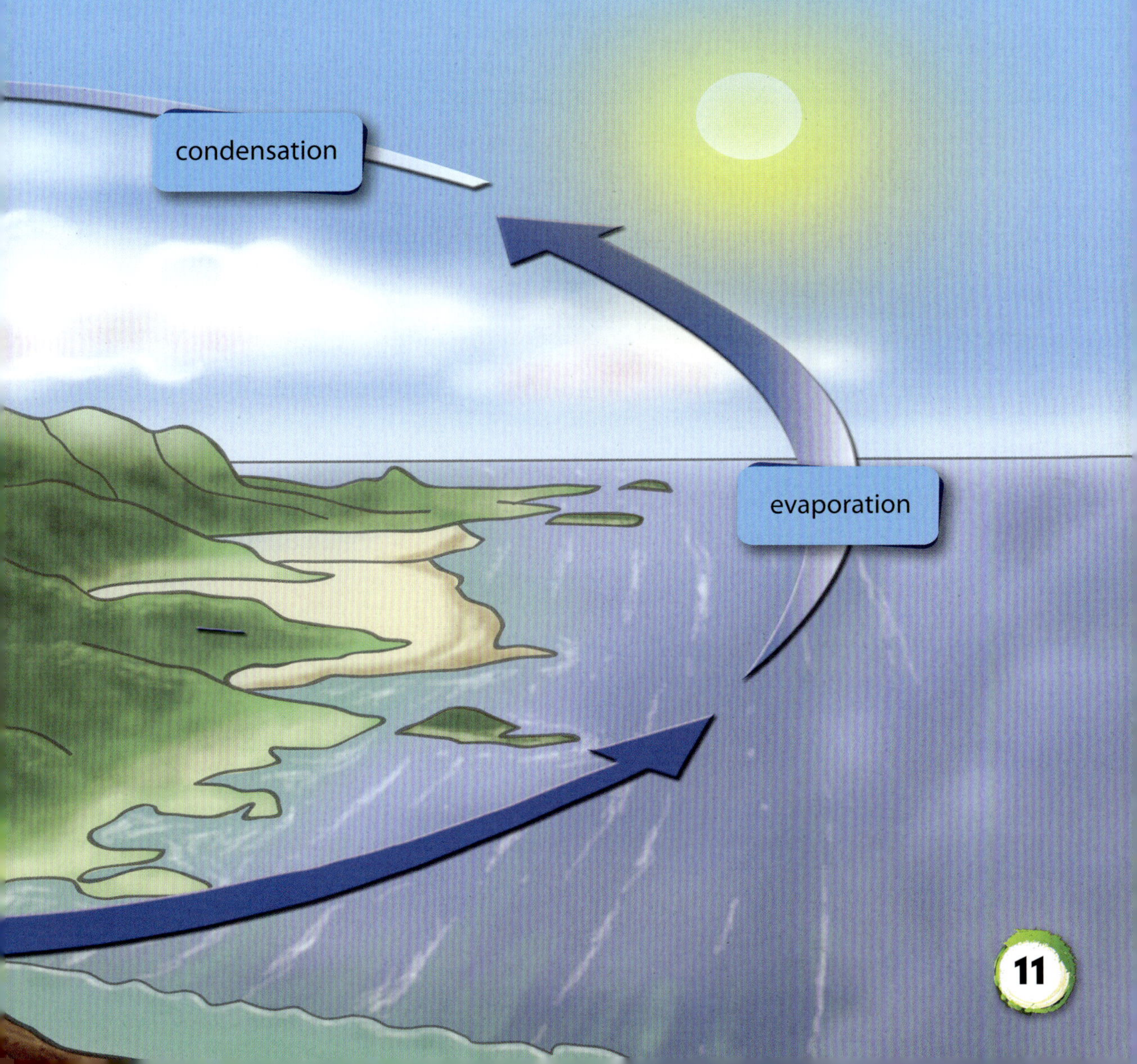

As clouds get colder, tiny drops of water form. Soon the drops fall from the clouds. Sometimes, they fall as rain. Other times, they fall as **hail**. If it is cold enough, they fall as snow! These are all types of precipitation.

Each snowflake is unique.

The water falls to Earth. It collects in lakes and rivers. It flows to the oceans. When the water warms up, the cycle starts again!

Wonderful Water

All living things need water. Plants need water to grow. They get water through their roots. Thin tubes carry the water up their stems. Water then passes through their leaves. It turns to vapor.

Animals need water, too! They must drink water to live.

Cats and Dogs

When a dog pants, water leaves its body as a vapor. Water can leave a cat's body through its nose!

water vapor
Water passes through the leaves and turns to vapor.
Water passes through the roots to the leaves.

Humans also need water to live. When you drink water, it moves through your body. It keeps you healthy. Some of the water leaves your body. This happens when you sweat and when you go to the bathroom.

This boy is drinking water to replace the water that he lost on a hot day.

See for Yourself

Breathe on a mirror. The mirror will fog up. The fog is the water vapor leaving your body.

We use water to grow plants to eat.

We use water in many ways. It is not just for drinking. We use water to clean things, including ourselves. We use water to grow food to eat. We use water to cook food. We also use water to make power. We can use that power to light our homes.

Each American uses nearly 100 gallons of water a day. Most of this is used to flush the toilet!

Dams hold back water. They run some of the water through pipes to run machines that make electricity.

Water is being used to cook these potatoes.

Saving Our Water

We need water to live. It is important that we do not waste it. There are many ways you can save water.

A faucet that drips just once per second wastes 27,000 gallons of water each year.

You can take shorter showers. You can turn the sink off while you brush your teeth. If you have a pipe that leaks, make sure you get it fixed right away!

This man fixes a leaky pipe to help save water.

This boy saves water by brushing his teeth with the faucet off.

We must keep our water clean. If it is dirty, we cannot use it. Factories may make water dirty. They may leak **chemicals** into it. This **pollutes** the water. Pollution makes water unsafe.

Oil may spill into the ocean. This hurts plants and animals that live there. Some may even die.

Be Careful!

Polluted water is not safe! It can make you very sick. Be sure to stay away from it.

A worker cleans a bird covered in oil.

Sometimes, unsafe gases get into the air. Power plants that use coal may make these gases. Old cars and factories may make these gases, too.

These gases mix with water vapor in the air. This makes **acid rain**. Acid rain then falls back to Earth. It pollutes the water. It can kill plants. And it can make animals sick.

Acid rain killed these plants and polluted the water.

Turn Off the Lights!

You can help reduce acid rain by turning off your lights. The less power you use, the less gases the power plants will put into the air.

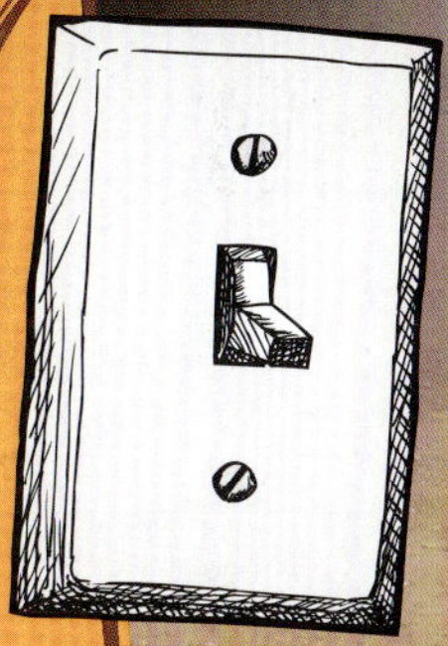

The water cycle never ends. It keeps going and going. This is a good thing since we need water to live! It is important to know how the water cycle works. This helps us know why we need to keep our water safe and clean.

Let's Do Science!

How can you observe the water cycle? See for yourself!

What to Get

- 2 mason jars (one with a lid)
- marker
- masking tape
- water

What to Do

1. Place a strip of tape down one side of each jar.

2. Fill both jars half way with water. Mark the water level on each piece of tape. Place the lid on one jar. Seal it tight. Leave the second jar open.

3. Let the jars sit in a sunny spot for two weeks. Then, look at the water level of each jar. What do you see? Explain what you think happened.

Glossary

acid rain—rain that contains dangerous chemicals caused by smoke from factories, power plants, and cars

chemicals—substances made from a chemical process

condensation—the process by which gas cools and becomes a liquid

evaporation—the process of changing from a liquid to a gas

hail—pieces of ice that fall from clouds

liquid—something that is able to flow freely, such as water

pollutes—makes dirty and unsafe

precipitation— Rain, snow, and other forms of water that fall to the ground

solid—something that is firm and hard, not liquid or gas

vapor—a liquid in the form of gas, or tiny drops of water mixed with air

Index

Your Turn!

Saving Water

Water is very important to all living things. We need water to live. Think of ways you can help save water and keep it clean. List all your ideas, and share them with your friends and family.